ALA Survey of Librarian Salaries 1994

Mary Jo Lynch, *Project Director*
Margaret Myers
Jeniece Guy

ALA Survey Report

Amercian Library Association
Office for Research and Statistics
Office for Library Personnel Resources

American Library Association
Chicago and London 1994

ISBN: 0-8389-7719-7
ISSN: 0747-7201

Copyright © 1994 by the American Library Association.
All rights reserved except those which may be granted by Sections 107
and 108 of the Copyright Revision Act of 1976.

Printed in the United States of America.

Acknowledgments

The authors wish to thank the many respondents who completed our questionnaires. Without their cooperation, this report would not be possible. We are grateful to the Association of Research Libraries (ARL) for sharing data with us as described in Appendix D and especially to Gordon Fretwell of the University of Massachusetts at Amherst who produced the data diskette. We are also grateful to Ed Lakner, Sylvia Temperley, Diane La Barbera and other staff at the Library Research Center of the Graduate School of Library and Information Science at the University of Illinois who managed the mailings and processed the returns. Finally, thanks are due to Stephanie Suh, Maxine Moore and Patricia Jackson for word processing the revised text and tables.

Table of Contents

Acknowledgments

Introduction 1

Results 3

    Director 4
    Deputy/Associate/Assistant Director 7
    Department Head/Branch Head 10
    Reference/Information Librarian 13
    Cataloger and/or Classifier 16
    Children's and/or Young Adult Services Librarian 19
    Beginning Librarian 21

Discussion

    Summary of Results 25
        Salaries by Position 25
        Salaries by Type of Library 26
        Salaries by Region of the U.S. 26

    Complicating Factors 27
        Meaning of "Full-Time" 27
        Meaning of "Professional" 27
        Salaries Below $19,000 28
        Job Levels or Faculty Ranks 28
        Longevity Pay 28
        Level of Experience 28

Appendixes

    A. Salary Surveys Providing Information on Library Workers 29
    B. ALA Policies Relating to Salary Issues 37
    C. Selected Bibliography on Compensation and Employee Benefits 41
    D. Technical Considerations 43
    E. Cover Letter 49
    F. Survey Questionnaire 51
    G. Salaries Paid for Less than a 12-month Year in Academic Libraries 55

Introduction

Librarians, the people who hire them, and interested others often ask the American Library Association (ALA) Office for Library Personnel Resources (OLPR) to tell them what salary might be paid to a librarian in a particular position, working in a particular type of library, in a particular part of the U.S. To fill the need for information of this kind, ALA began conducting a periodic survey of salaries for full-time professionals in academic and public libraries. Reports were published biennially from 1982 to 1988 and became annual in 1989.

This report, the tenth in a series, presents salaries paid to incumbents in six positions commonly found in U.S. academic and public libraries. Salaries were reported as of April 1, 1994. For each of five positions, the report contains six tables, one for each of five library types and one for all five combined. The sixth position--children's and/or young adult services librarian--is shown only for public libraries. Each of the tables shows the range, mean, first quartile, median, and third quartile of salaries in four geographic regions. Salaries paid to beginning professionals are also displayed in the same way.

The 1994 report shares the following characteristics with its immediate predecessor:

- It is based on a survey of **libraries**, not individual librarians.

- It is based on a survey of **full-time** positions.

- It is based on a survey of **public and academic** libraries only. (Sources for salaries in other libraries are given in Appendix A.)

- The public and academic library universe is stratified by the same **type/size criteria**: public libraries serving populations of from 25,000 to 99,999, public libraries serving populations of 100,000 or more, two-year colleges, four-year colleges, and universities. (The last category includes all institutions offering work beyond the bachelor's level).

- The nation is stratified into the same **geographic areas**: North Atlantic, Great Lakes and Plains, Southeast, West and Southwest (see Appendix D for list of states).

- It shows the **first quartile, median, and third quartile** for salaries paid in each type/size of library and region in addition to the **mean and range** (low and high) for each position reported.

- It shows salaries paid to staff **with master's degrees from graduate library education programs accredited by ALA**.

- It shows salaries for **beginning librarians** in both public and academic libraries.

- It shows salaries for **five positions in both public and academic libraries** (Director, Deputy/Associate/Assistant Director, Department Head/Branch Head, Reference/Information Librarian, Cataloger and/or Classifier), and **one position in public libraries only** (Children's and/or Young Adult Services Librarian).

The 1994 survey also contained five questions asked on a one-time-only basis:

1. Is there a single position on your staff with primary responsibility for many or all of the following duties related to library technology?
   - Recommend policies for automation
   - Plan for the installation of a system
   - Evaluate/select system hardware/software
   - Work with agencies outside the library
   - Test the installed systems
   - Plan site preparation (space, electric, A/C, etc.)
   - Evaluate systems/applications software
   - Trouble shoot system malfunctions
   - Install/configure hardware/software
   - Document system implementation, changes, etc.
   - Oversee the daily operation of the system
   - Participate in the preparation of an RFP
   - Analyze system/user interaction
   - Authorize expenditures for hardware/software

   _____ Yes (please continue)
   _____ No (please skip to A below)

2. What is the title of this position?

3. Is the position one of the following:
   _____ Deputy/Associate/Assistant Director
   _____ Department Head
   _____ none of the above

4. Does the current incumbent have a master's degree from a program accredited by ALA?
   ___Yes ___No

5. What annual salary is paid to the current incumbent? $_____ per year

Of the 963 respondents who answered question 1, more than half (51.6 percent) answered "yes". Of those 497 respondents, 72 indicated that the Director or Head Librarian performed the specified duties, 143 indicated that they were performed by some other traditional managerial position (e.g., head of technical services), and 265 reported a specialized title that included such words as "automation," "computer," "systems." The remaining 17 did not respond to question 2 ("title of this position"). Additional details will appear in a forthcoming issue of *Library Personnel News*.

The Library Research Center of the University of Illinois Graduate School of Library and Information Science performed the mailing, processing, and computer analysis of the questionnaires. Mary Jo Lynch, Director of ALA's Office for Research and Statistics (ORS), directed the project and wrote this report with assistance from Margaret Myers, Director of ALA's Office for Library Personnel Resources (OLPR) and Jeniece Guy, OLPR Assistant Director. Myers was responsible for Appendix A, B, and C.

We hope the results of the survey will be useful to employers of librarians who need this information in administering an equitable pay plan and to librarians seeking employment or career advancement.

Results

The survey questionnaire was mailed to 1,245 randomly selected libraries on March 31, 1994. Samples were drawn from twenty groups of libraries formed by stratifying five type-of-library categories by four regions of the U. S. Appendix D describes how groups were formed and sampled. By the second week in June, useable responses had been received from 964 libraries, 77.4 percent of those sampled.

The results of this survey are presented on the following pages in seven sets of tables. The first five sets present salaries paid to incumbents in positions common to both public and academic libraries. Respondents were asked to report all full-time incumbents *with master's degrees from graduate library education programs accredited by ALA* except for beginning professionals, whose salaries are shown in a special table. There are three pages of tables for each position. The first table presents salaries paid in medium-sized public libraries, i.e., those serving between 25,000 and 99,999. For each of four regions of the country and for the nation as a whole, the table shows the number of positions reported (N), the lowest salary and the highest salary (range), the mean (arithmetic average), the first quartile, median, and third quartile. This pattern is repeated for large public libraries (i.e., those serving populations of 100,000 or more), and for libraries in two-year colleges, four-year colleges, and in universities (i.e., institutions offering work beyond the baccalaureate degree).

Following these five sets of tables is a smaller set for children's and/or young adult services librarian. For this position, tables are given only for the two sizes of public libraries and for all public libraries.

The last set of tables describes salaries paid to beginning professionals following the pattern set in the first six sets of tables.

The following example illustrates how to interpret the tables. In the first table for the position of director--the table presenting salaries paid in medium-sized public libraries--there were 84 salaries reported from the North Atlantic region. The lowest of these was $31,500 and the highest was $113,200. When all the salaries were added together and the result was divided by the total number (84) the average or mean was $55,223. When all the salaries were arrayed from low to high, 25 percent of them fell below $43,529, the first quartile, 50 percent fell below $51,730, the median, and 50 percent were above $51,730. Seventy-five percent fell below $61,527, the third quartile, and 25 percent were above that amount. The middle 50 percent of the salaries fell between $43,529 and $61,527.

Two caveats should be observed in reading the tables. The higher the number of cases (N), the more reliable the results of the sample in giving a true picture of the total population. When the number of cases is less than twenty-five, the results should be used with caution. This caution is especially applicable to the regional data for libraries where the number of professional staff is often small-- medium sized public libraries, four-year colleges, and two-year colleges. Another caveat is that when the mean and the median are not close together, the mean is being influenced by some unusual values. When the mean is much higher than the median, there are several very high salaries. When the mean is much lower than the median, there are several very low salaries.

Director
(Page 1 of 3)

Chief administrative officer of the library or library system. Plans and directs all aspects of the operation. May have job title such as Librarian or Head Librarian.

Medium-sized Public Library
(Serving a population of from 25,000 to 99,999)

	MEAN	FIRST QUARTILE	MEDIAN	THIRD QUARTILE
North Atlantic N=84 Range= $31,500-$113,200	55,223	43,529	51,730	61,527
Great Lakes & Plains N=82 Range= $25,360-$83,028	49,763	41,111	48,926	57,343
Southeast N=48 Range= $25,400-$60,476	39,733	34,208	38,042	43,706
West & Southwest N=45 Range= $28,936-$107,000	56,279	42,600	54,972	65,760
All Regions N=259 Range= $25,360-$113,200	50,807	40,000	48,410	58,000

Large Public Library
(Serving a population of 100,000 or more)

	MEAN	FIRST QUARTILE	MEDIAN	THIRD QUARTILE
North Atlantic N=26 Range= $36,400-$97,850	68,849	52,562	68,929	82,742
Great Lakes & Plains N=40 Range= $37,960-$98,700	69,520	56,150	67,900	83,750
Southeast N=48 Range= $30,615-$103,896	59,559	48,448	55,417	68,217
West & Southwest N=55 Range= $36,504-$107,651	72,453	59,688	74,892	85,000
All Regions N=169 Range= $30,615-$107,651	67,542	52,562	67,360	81,885

SOURCE: ALA SURVEY OF LIBRARIAN SALARIES, 1994

Director (Page 2 of 3)

Chief administrative officer of the library or library system. Plans and directs all aspects of the operation. May have job title such as Librarian or Head Librarian.

Two-Year College

	MEAN	FIRST QUARTILE	MEDIAN	THIRD QUARTILE
North Atlantic N=34 Range=$24,000-$75,215	48,874	40,494	50,826	57,565
Great Lakes & Plains N=30 Range=$22,667-$71,698	48,261	42,000	46,358	54,360
Southeast N=38 Range= $24,000-$62,000	41,579	32,500	42,542	49,000
West & Southwest N=28 Range= $31,572-$70,667	47,068	39,884	45,064	52,905
All Regions N=130 Range= $22,667-$75,215	46,211	39,000	45,317	52,942

Four-Year College

	MEAN	FIRST QUARTILE	MEDIAN	THIRD QUARTILE
North Atlantic N=36 Range=$25,000-$78,300	50,986	39,500	50,173	59,540
Great Lakes & Plains N=33 Range=$24,000-$75,000	43,476	34,000	37,215	54,570
Southeast N=27 Range=$22,000-$62,000	40,555	30,152	41,333	48,200
West & Southwest N=24 Range=$20,000-$79,248	41,521	30,100	40,941	48,608
All Regions N=120 Range= $20,000-$79,248	44,681	34,050	42,000	54,594

SOURCE: ALA SURVEY OF LIBRARIAN SALARIES, 1994

Director (Page 3 of 3)

Chief administrative officer of the library or library system. Plans and directs all aspects of the operation. May have job title such as Librarian or Head Librarian.

University

	MEAN	FIRST QUARTILE	MEDIAN	THIRD QUARTILE
North Atlantic N=65 Range=$25,000-$142,000	66,030	50,000	65,124	76,490
Great Lakes & Plains N=59 Range=$28,500-$118,625	59,781	39,000	57,304	75,000
Southeast N=59 Range=$26,600-$104,000	60,901	44,266	61,267	72,743
West & Southwest N=57 Range=$30,800-$118,000	65,820	50,000	67,634	80,340
All Regions N=240 Range=$25,000-$142,000	63,183	45,944	62,249	76,451

All Academic and Public Libraries

	MEAN	FIRST QUARTILE	MEDIAN	THIRD QUARTILE
North Atlantic N=245 Range=$24,000-$142,000	58,032	45,000	54,495	68,295
Great Lakes & Plains N=244 Range=$22,667-$118,625	54,389	40,255	51,806	63,301
Southeast N=220 Range=$22,000-$104,000	50,155	38,000	46,690	59,773
West & Southwest N=209 Range=$20,000-$118,000	60,209	43,599	56,848	75,000
All Regions N=918 Range=$20,000-$142,000	55,672	41,780	52,310	67,122

SOURCE: ALA SURVEY OF LIBRARIAN SALARIES, 1994

Deputy/Associate/Assistant Director
(Page 1 of 3)

Aids Director in planning and directing some or all aspects of library or library system. May manage a major aspect of the library operation (e.g., technical services, public services, collection development, systems/automation).

Medium-sized Public Library
(Serving a population of from 25,000 to 99,999)

	MEAN	FIRST QUARTILE	MEDIAN	THIRD QUARTILE
North Atlantic N=51 Range=$26,133-$77,320	42,767	35,100	41,766	50,407
Great Lakes & Plains N=55 Range=$22,863-$73,313	38,582	31,560	37,284	45,500
Southeast N=31 Range=$21,000-$39,800	31,354	27,654	30,161	36,270
West & Southwest N=27 Range=$28,376-$85,800	44,158	33,460	38,088	51,000
All Regions N=164 Range=$21,000-$85,800	39,435	31,430	37,045	45,423

Large Public Library
(Serving a population of 100,000 or more)

	MEAN	FIRST QUARTILE	MEDIAN	THIRD QUARTILE
North Atlantic N=62 Range=$32,061-$77,896	57,690	47,459	59,566	66,040
Great Lakes & Plains N=53 Range=$26,000-$83,688	54,599	43,600	56,051	65,283
Southeast N=104 Range=$28,644-$72,486	47,431	38,899	46,064	54,470
West & Southwest N=101 Range=$29,364-$87,717	56,193	48,626	56,125	63,037
All Regions N=320 Range=$26,000-$87,717	53,372	43,616	53,256	62,759

SOURCE: ALA SURVEY OF LIBRARIAN SALARIES, 1994

Deputy/Associate/Assistant Director (Page 2 of 3)

Aids Director in planning and directing some or all aspects of library or library system. May manage a major aspect of the library operation (e.g., technical services, public services, collection development, systems/automation).

Two-Year College

	MEAN	FIRST QUARTILE	MEDIAN	THIRD QUARTILE
North Atlantic N=8 Range=$27,000-$69,000	40,546	31,620	36,556	46,010
Great Lakes & Plains N=3 Range=$27,500-$62,272	43,091	27,500	39,500	62,272
Southeast N=13 Range=$23,964-$44,400	33,482	26,000	31,690	42,000
West & Southwest N=11 Range=$28,587-$68,000	40,630	30,000	36,500	54,624
All Regions N=35 Range=$23,964-$69,000	38,167	30,000	34,000	42,533

Four-Year College

	MEAN	FIRST QUARTILE	MEDIAN	THIRD QUARTILE
North Atlantic N=14 Range=$28,000-$56,400	40,236	35,905	39,775	44,308
Great Lakes & Plains N=9 Range=$20,976-$50,324	31,873	25,000	27,500	36,000
Southeast N=8 Range=$15,000-$40,000	29,602	25,406	30,000	35,500
West & Southwest N=12 Range=$21,862-$64,872	31,983	24,845	29,400	32,927
All Regions N=43 Range=$15,000-$64,872	34,204	27,050	32,200	39,850

SOURCE: ALA SURVEY OF LIBRARIAN SALARIES, 1994

Deputy/Associate/Assistant Director (Page 3 of 3)

Aids Director in planning and directing some or all aspects of library or library system. May manage a major aspect of the library operation (e.g., technical services, public services, collection development, systems/automation).

University

	MEAN	FIRST QUARTILE	MEDIAN	THIRD QUARTILE
North Atlantic N=99 Range=$22,000-$105,000	55,465	46,082	53,928	64,851
Great Lakes & Plains N=76 Range=$23,795-$78,500	50,152	40,626	49,427	58,545
Southeast N=80 Range=$26,737-$70,000	47,756	39,612	47,175	55,050
West & Southwest N=79 Range=$28,648-$90,521	52,182	42,108	49,000	61,296
All Regions N=334 Range=$22,000-$105,000	51,633	42,370	49,979	59,935

All Academic and Public Libraries

	MEAN	FIRST QUARTILE	MEDIAN	THIRD QUARTILE
North Atlantic N=234 Range=$22,000-$105,000	51,866	41,600	50,199	61,898
Great Lakes & Plains N=196 Range=$20,976-$83,688	47,160	36,681	45,755	57,510
Southeast N=236 Range=$15,000-$72,486	44,057	34,935	42,897	52,938
West & Southwest N=230 Range=$21,862-$90,521	51,395	41,236	50,522	61,207
All Regions N=896 Range=$15,000-$105,000	48,659	38,307	47,249	58,443

SOURCE: ALA SURVEY OF LIBRARIAN SALARIES, 1994

Department Head/Branch Head
(Page 1 of 3)

Manages operation of a library unit that is physically separate from the main library (e.g., a branch or a department library) or of one aspect of the main library (e.g., Reference Department, Serials Department, Children's Department).

Medium-sized Public Library
(Serving a population of from 25,000 to 99,999)

	MEAN	FIRST QUARTILE	MEDIAN	THIRD QUARTILE
North Atlantic N=151 Range=$16,300-$68,325	39,497	30,860	37,579	46,161
Great Lakes & Plains N=168 Range=$20,000-$51,382	34,276	28,544	33,211	39,134
Southeast N=55 Range=$14,000-$43,497	29,504	24,636	29,010	33,254
West & Southwest N=70 Range=$20,176-$60,638	40,762	34,486	41,712	45,325
All Regions N=444 Range=$14,000-$68,325	36,483	28,769	34,605	42,982

Large Public Library
(Serving a population of 100,000 or more)

	MEAN	FIRST QUARTILE	MEDIAN	THIRD QUARTILE
North Atlantic N=487 Range=$18,000-$69,389	42,869	37,402	43,645	48,443
Great Lakes & Plains N=496 Range=$20,342-$68,907	41,170	35,000	41,028	45,944
Southeast N=395 Range=$21,576-$60,163	36,463	29,307	36,120	42,384
West & Southwest N=504 Range=$20,016-$79,682	42,814	35,910	42,456	49,696
All Regions N=1,882 Range=$18,000-$79,682	41,062	34,628	41,051	46,672

SOURCE: ALA SURVEY OF LIBRARIAN SALARIES, 1994

Department Head/Branch Head (Page 2 of 3)

Manages operation of a library unit that is physically separate from the main library (e.g., a branch or a department library) or of one aspect of the main library (e.g., Reference Department, Serials Department, Children's Department).

Two-Year College

	MEAN	FIRST QUARTILE	MEDIAN	THIRD QUARTILE
North Atlantic N=31 Range=$28,600-$89,413	47,720	36,000	43,618	59,386
Great Lakes & Plains N=5 Range=$20,000-$74,405	36,459	25,318	26,600	35,972
Southeast N=18 Range=$21,000-$49,000	35,579	30,000	35,016	41,352
West & Southwest N=13 Range=$24,426-$53,333	41,618	36,293	43,824	44,346
All Regions N=67 Range=$20,000-$89,413	42,434	34,000	41,136	48,000

Four-Year College

	MEAN	FIRST QUARTILE	MEDIAN	THIRD QUARTILE
North Atlantic N=38 Range=$24,000-$69,600	39,746	33,500	38,613	44,515
Great Lakes & Plains N=19 Range=$21,000-$59,622	38,484	29,383	36,749	47,438
Southeast N=20 Range=$12,000-$51,296	32,370	28,300	29,906	37,615
West & Southwest N=18 Range=$19,500-$58,600	37,311	26,518	31,326	51,264
All Regions N=95 Range=$12,000-$69,600	37,479	29,355	36,000	44,515

SOURCE: ALA SURVEY OF LIBRARIAN SALARIES, 1994

Department Head/Branch Head (Page 3 of 3)

Manages operation of a library unit that is physically separate from the main library (e.g., a branch or a department library) or of one aspect of the main library (e.g., Reference Department, Serials Department, Children's Department).

University

	MEAN	FIRST QUARTILE	MEDIAN	THIRD QUARTILE
North Atlantic N=345 Range=$18,450-$107,120	42,546	37,069	41,655	47,600
Great Lakes & Plains N=273 Range=$22,032-$81,535	41,015	33,420	38,748	47,086
Southeast N=286 Range=$22,270-$70,780	36,746	31,765	36,143	41,500
West & Southwest N=279 Range=$21,487-$136,736	45,056	35,562	44,592	51,134
All Regions N=1,183 Range=$18,450-$136,736	41,383	34,000	39,827	46,760

All Academic and Public Libraries

	MEAN	FIRST QUARTILE	MEDIAN	THIRD QUARTILE
North Atlantic N=1052 Range=$16,300-$107,120	42,310	36,000	42,264	47,776
Great Lakes & Plains N=961 Range=$20,000-$81,535	39,843	32,968	38,955	45,712
Southeast N=774 Range=$12,000-$70,780	35,947	29,893	35,381	41,137
West & Southwest N=884 Range=$19,500-$136,736	43,230	35,480	42,456	49,776
All Regions N=3671 Range=$12,000-$136,736	40,544	33,446	39,876	46,375

SOURCE: ALA SURVEY OF LIBRARIAN SALARIES, 1994

Reference/Information Librarian
(Page 1 of 3)

Locates information for library users or helps users find it in print materials, automated databases, or other sources. Answers questions and gives instruction about the use of the library. Selects materials for the reference collection and general collections.

Medium-sized Public Library
(Serving a population of from 25,000 to 99,999)

	MEAN	FIRST QUARTILE	MEDIAN	THIRD QUARTILE
North Atlantic N=140 Range=$17,150-$66,789	35,591	28,895	33,634	40,334
Great Lakes & Plains N=132 Range=$19,200-$46,347	29,729	25,095	29,312	33,475
Southeast N=32 Range=$13,000-$36,805	24,992	21,750	24,843	27,357
West & Southwest N=64 Range=$22,672-$48,560	33,756	28,559	34,042	39,277
All Regions N=368 Range=$13,000-$66,789	32,247	26,306	31,359	36,298

Large Public Library
(Serving a population of 100,000 or more)

	MEAN	FIRST QUARTILE	MEDIAN	THIRD QUARTILE
North Atlantic N=575 Range=$17,300-$55,777	34,625	30,368	35,591	37,181
Great Lakes & Plains N=461 Range=$20,000-$48,714	33,362	29,016	32,656	37,843
Southeast N=324 Range=$19,281-$48,152	30,119	25,165	28,953	33,925
West & Southwest N=626 Range=$20,016-$55,728	35,513	30,648	35,305	39,780
All Regions N=1,986 Range=$17,300-$55,777	33,877	29,127	33,603	37,960

SOURCE: ALA SURVEY OF LIBRARIAN SALARIES, 1994

Reference/Information Librarian (Page 2 of 3)

Locates information for library users or helps users find it in print materials, automated databases, or other sources. Answers questions and gives instruction about the use of the library. Selects materials for the reference collection and general collections.

Two-Year College

	MEAN	FIRST QUARTILE	MEDIAN	THIRD QUARTILE
North Atlantic N=49 Range=$22,885-$84,155	45,435	33,894	43,000	50,773
Great Lakes & Plains N=30 Range=$21,000-$87,161	49,656	34,729	49,727	64,024
Southeast N=38 Range=$20,000-$53,864	38,730	33,129	38,500	44,436
West & Southwest N=39 Range=$21,508-$60,367	41,082	32,608	41,544	50,304
All Regions N=156 Range=$20,000-$87,161	43,525	34,100	41,563	50,720

Four-Year College

	MEAN	FIRST QUARTILE	MEDIAN	THIRD QUARTILE
North Atlantic N=44 Range=$17,500-$49,130	31,132	26,306	31,023	35,840
Great Lakes & Plains N=37 Range=$21,000-$51,275	32,630	26,880	30,000	35,713
Southeast N=27 Range=$19,000-$43,680	27,694	23,300	27,000	29,333
West & Southwest N=21 Range=$19,000-$62,700	32,355	27,000	28,080	36,898
All Regions N=129 Range=$17,500-$62,700	31,041	25,744	28,970	35,200

SOURCE: ALA SURVEY OF LIBRARIAN SALARIES, 1994

Reference/Information Librarian (Page 3 of 3)

Locates information for library users or helps users find it in print materials, automated databases, or other sources. Answers questions and gives instruction about the use of the library. Selects materials for the reference collection and general collections.

University

	MEAN	FIRST QUARTILE	MEDIAN	THIRD QUARTILE
North Atlantic N=288 Range=$20,900-$61,164	35,596	29,965	34,633	41,086
Great Lakes & Plains N=265 Range=$20,000-$62,832	34,223	28,069	32,817	38,360
Southeast N=233 Range=$21,008-$48,261	30,596	26,512	30,000	33,500
West & Southwest N=276 Range=$22,000-$73,700	37,335	28,401	34,497	43,824
All Regions N=1,062 Range=$20,000-$73,700	34,608	28,000	32,515	38,948

All Academic and Public Libraries

	MEAN	FIRST QUARTILE	MEDIAN	THIRD QUARTILE
North Atlantic N=1,096 Range=$17,150-$84,155	35,347	29,758	34,875	38,164
Great Lakes & Plains N=925 Range=$19,200-$87,161	33,589	28,236	32,094	37,843
Southeast N=654 Range=$13,000-$53,864	30,438	25,472	29,327	34,078
West & Southwest N=1,026 Range=$19,000-$73,700	36,040	29,878	34,801	40,807
All Regions N=3,701 Range=$13,000-$87,161	34,233	28,398	33,057	38,231

SOURCE: ALA SURVEY OF LIBRARIAN SALARIES, 1994

Cataloger and/or Classifier
(Page 1 of 3)

Organizes all types of material purchased by the library. Describes each item in standard format and assigns access points. Assigns subject headings and classification numbers. May use automated systems. May be involved with only descriptive cataloging or only subject cataloging/classification.

Medium-sized Public Library
(Serving a population of from 25,000 to 99,999)

	MEAN	FIRST QUARTILE	MEDIAN	THIRD QUARTILE
North Atlantic N=30 Range=$21,000-$59,043	33,892	27,780	32,350	39,507
Great Lakes & Plains N=37 Range=$18,886-$43,680	29,038	24,504	28,572	32,100
Southeast N=12 Range=$18,999-$47,574	27,680	22,344	24,965	32,921
West & Southwest N=27 Range=$19,600-$48,560	33,439	27,498	34,328	37,910
All Regions N=106 Range=$18,886-$59,043	31,379	25,000	30,074	36,399

Large Public Library
(Serving a population of 100,000 or more)

	MEAN	FIRST QUARTILE	MEDIAN	THIRD QUARTILE
North Atlantic N=48 Range=$21,400-$52,582	34,718	29,758	33,468	40,185
Great Lakes & Plains N=57 Range=$22,050-$54,444	33,953	28,271	33,571	37,843
Southeast N=56 Range=$19,050-$56,649	31,583	26,428	30,586	36,386
West & Southwest N=91 Range=$20,016-$50,124	35,510	30,648	34,263	40,486
All Regions N=252 Range=$19,050-$56,649	34,134	28,848	33,820	38,991

SOURCE: ALA SURVEY OF LIBRARIAN SALARIES, 1994

Cataloger and/or Classifier (Page 2 of 3)

Organizes all types of material purchased by the library. Describes each item in standard format and assigns access points. Assigns subject headings and classification numbers. May use automated systems. May be involved with only descriptive cataloging or only subject cataloging/classification.

Two-Year College

	MEAN	FIRST QUARTILE	MEDIAN	THIRD QUARTILE
North Atlantic N=18 Range=$24,500-$67,088	48,010	35,263	46,262	60,507
Great Lakes & Plains N=15 Range=$30,427-$70,580	48,963	35,000	48,875	60,484
Southeast N=13 Range=$20,241-$45,000	31,827	24,950	31,130	37,823
West & Southwest N=16 Range=$22,352-$57,600	41,102	30,194	42,666	50,152
All Regions N=62 Range=$20,241-$70,580	43,065	31,130	42,334	54,188

Four-Year College

	MEAN	FIRST QUARTILE	MEDIAN	THIRD QUARTILE
North Atlantic N=23 Range=$22,312-$58,911	33,477	26,945	31,500	38,400
Great Lakes & Plains N=20 Range=$20,000-$35,735	28,194	25,373	28,250	30,841
Southeast N=17 Range=$20,400-$47,280	28,955	25,000	27,100	29,329
West & Southwest N=9 Range=$24,000-$42,500	31,934	25,135	35,415	36,024
All Regions N=69 Range=$20,000-$58,911	30,630	25,745	28,861	35,000

SOURCE: ALA SURVEY OF LIBRARIAN SALARIES, 1994

Cataloger and/or Classifier (Page 3 of 3)

Organizes all types of material purchased by the library. Describes each item in standard format and assigns access points. Assigns subject headings and classification numbers. May use automated systems. May be involved with only descriptive cataloging or only subject cataloging/classification.

University

	MEAN	FIRST QUARTILE	MEDIAN	THIRD QUARTILE
North Atlantic N=128 Range=$20,000-$56,115	34,832	30,495	33,532	38,070
Great Lakes & Plains N=120 Range=$21,100-$57,096	33,292	27,063	31,976	37,605
Southeast N=119 Range=$21,000-$47,325	29,616	26,110	28,400	33,132
West & Southwest N=131 Range=$23,000-$63,948	36,625	29,190	35,800	41,829
All Regions N=498 Range=$20,000-$63,948	33,686	28,000	32,319	37,644

All Academic and Public Libraries

	MEAN	FIRST QUARTILE	MEDIAN	THIRD QUARTILE
North Atlantic N=247 Range=$20,000-$67,088	35,530	29,758	33,675	40,250
Great Lakes & Plains N=249 Range=$18,886-$70,580	33,346	27,000	31,536	37,132
Southeast N=217 Range=$18,999-$56,649	30,097	25,836	28,896	33,800
West & Southwest N=274 Range=$19,600-$63,948	36,048	29,750	34,880	41,565
All Regions N=987 Range=$18,886-$70,580	33,928	27,839	32,400	38,404

SOURCE: ALA SURVEY OF LIBRARIAN SALARIES, 1994

Children's and/or Young Adult Services Librarian
(Page 1 of 2)

Plans and conducts library services for children and/or young adults. Advises on reading materials. Selects materials for the collection. May plan and conduct special programs and outreach services.

Medium-sized Public Library
(Serving a population of from 25,000 to 99,999)

	MEAN	FIRST QUARTILE	MEDIAN	THIRD QUARTILE
North Atlantic N=92 Range=$17,550-$58,085	34,600	28,871	33,828	39,496
Great Lakes & Plains N=57 Range=$19,200-$42,957	28,256	24,262	28,071	32,000
Southeast N=23 Range=$15,000-$39,273	26,384	21,989	24,470	32,579
West & Southwest N=38 Range=$20,176-$49,944	35,191	30,000	36,246	40,142
All Regions N=210 Range=$15,000-$58,085	32,085	26,042	31,484	36,528

Large Public Library
(Serving a population of 100,000 or more)

	MEAN	FIRST QUARTILE	MEDIAN	THIRD QUARTILE
North Atlantic N=196 Range=$16,000-$53,199	35,350	29,868	34,593	39,491
Great Lakes & Plains N=228 Range=$19,204-$56,082	32,227	28,335	31,128	36,086
Southeast N=112 Range=$19,281-$41,123	29,266	24,471	28,113	33,676
West & Southwest N=324 Range=$20,016-$67,272	35,947	31,264	36,379	39,564
All Regions N=860 Range=$16,000-$67,272	33,954	29,365	33,144	38,917

SOURCE: ALA SURVEY OF LIBRARIAN SALARIES, 1994

Children's and/or Young Adult Services Librarian (Page 2 of 2)

Plans and conducts library services for children and/or young adults. Advises on reading materials. Selects materials for the collection. May plan and conduct special programs and outreach services.

All Public Libraries

	MEAN	FIRST QUARTILE	MEDIAN	THIRD QUARTILE
North Atlantic N=288 Range=$16,000-$58,085	35,110	29,766	34,223	39,491
Great Lakes & Plains N=285 Range=$19,200-$56,082	31,433	27,456	30,624	34,872
Southeast N=135 Range=$15,000-$41,123	28,775	23,850	27,624	33,309
West & Southwest N=362 Range=$20,016-$67,272	35,867	31,264	36,329	39,564
All Regions N=1,070 Range=$15,000-$67,272	33,588	28,773	32,888	38,732

Beginning Librarian

(Page 1 of 3)

Full-time staff member with a master's degree from a graduate library education program accredited by ALA, but no professional experience.

Medium-sized Public Library
(Serving a population of from 25,000 to 99,999)

	MEAN	FIRST QUARTILE	MEDIAN	THIRD QUARTILE
North Atlantic N=18 Range=$16,000-$29,505	24,621	22,149	24,979	27,570
Great Lakes & Plains N=17 Range=$17,950-$32,640	24,934	21,840	26,000	28,050
Southeast N=16 Range=$15,000-$27,654	22,960	21,750	22,773	26,309
West & Southwest N=5 Range=$21,998-$32,424	28,550	25,104	31,505	31,720
All Regions N=56 Range=$15,000-$32,640	24,592	21,999	24,448	27,471

Large Public Library
(Serving a population of 100,000 or more)

	MEAN	FIRST QUARTILE	MEDIAN	THIRD QUARTILE
North Atlantic N=97 Range=$22,036-$33,891	28,450	28,516	28,806	28,806
Great Lakes & Plains N=38 Range=$18,900-$28,880	25,056	22,345	25,696	26,726
Southeast N=44 Range=$19,281-$29,587	23,739	22,187	23,256	25,673
West & Southwest N=38 Range=$18,012-$34,442	27,225	24,240	26,844	30,000
All Regions N=217 Range=$18,012-$34,442	26,686	24,240	26,770	28,806

SOURCE: ALA SURVEY OF LIBRARIAN SALARIES, 1994

Beginning Librarian (Page 2 of 3)

Full-time staff member with a master's degree from a graduate library education program accredited by ALA, but no professional experience.

Two-Year College

	MEAN	FIRST QUARTILE	MEDIAN	THIRD QUARTILE
North Atlantic N=5 Range=$22,581-$37,000	28,681	23,700	28,808	31,314
Great Lakes & Plains N=0 Range=NA	NA	NA	NA	NA
Southeast N=9 Range=$21,500-$52,800	37,734	25,000	40,800	49,200
West & Southwest N=4 Range=$15,000-$32,449	24,737	18,750	25,750	30,725
All Regions N=18 Range=$15,000-$52,800	32,331	23,700	29,055	40,800

Four-Year College

	MEAN	FIRST QUARTILE	MEDIAN	THIRD QUARTILE
North Atlantic N=7 Range=$23,900-$37,920	27,974	25,000	26,000	30,000
Great Lakes & Plains N=6 Range=$21,500-$33,449	27,291	23,500	28,250	28,800
Southeast N=5 Range=$22,000-$24,000	23,160	22,800	23,000	24,000
West & Southwest N=6 Range=$19,000-$29,754	24,100	21,000	23,923	27,000
All Regions N=24 Range=$19,000-$37,920	25,832	23,000	24,923	28,250

SOURCE: ALA SURVEY OF LIBRARIAN SALARIES, 1994

Beginning Librarian (Page 3 of 3)

Full-time staff member with a master's degree from a graduate library education program accredited by ALA, but no professional experience.

University

	MEAN	FIRST QUARTILE	MEDIAN	THIRD QUARTILE
North Atlantic N=37 Range=$21,000-$48,800	27,834	26,000	27,136	29,000
Great Lakes & Plains N=41 Range=$18,996-$33,000	26,299	24,440	25,608	29,587
Southeast N=25 Range=$22,000-$33,000	25,375	23,970	25,000	26,500
West & Southwest N=30 Range=$21,000-$35,000	26,115	24,012	26,000	28,000
All Regions N=133 Range=$18,996-$48,800	26,511	24,440	26,000	28,840

All Academic and Public Libraries

	MEAN	FIRST QUARTILE	MEDIAN	THIRD QUARTILE
North Atlantic N=164 Range=$16,000-$48,800	27,878	26,538	28,806	28,806
Great Lakes & Plains N=102 Range=$17,950-$33,449	25,667	23,382	26,052	28,800
Southeast N=99 Range=$15,000-$52,800	25,269	22,500	24,000	26,500
West & Southwest N=83 Range=$15,000-$35,000	26,558	24,012	26,211	29,370
All Regions N=448 Range=$15,000-$52,800	26,553	24,000	26,576	28,806

SOURCE: ALA SURVEY OF LIBRARIAN SALARIES, 1994

Discussion

Summary of Results

People interested in a particular type of library or a particular type of work, or a particular region will have their own way of drawing conclusions from the results of this survey. However, the results may be summarized in a very general way by observing mean salaries paid to particular positions, mean salaries paid by particular types of libraries, or mean salaries paid in particular parts of the U.S.

Salaries by Position

The six positions are shown in rank order by mean of salaries paid on Table 1. Two additional columns are also given: a column showing the dollar amount of change from 1993 to 1994 and a column indicating the percent of increase.

Table 1. Rank Order of Position Titles by Mean of Salaries Paid

Title	94 Salary	93 Salary	Change Amount	%
Director	55,672	53,331	+2,341	+4.39
Deputy/Associate/Assistant Director	48,659	47,070	+1,589	+3.38
Department Head/Branch Head	40,544	39,352	+1,192	+3.03
Reference/Information Librarian	34,233	33,001	+1,232	+3.73
Cataloger and/or Classifier	33,928	32,582	+1,346	+4.13
Children's and/or Young Adult Services Librarian	33,588	32,530	+1,058	+3.25

SOURCE: ALA SURVEY OF LIBRARIAN SALARIES, 1994

The average of the percent of increase over the past year is 3.65 percent. The figure is slightly higher than the increase in comparable occupations reported by the U.S. Bureau of Labor Statistics (BLS) in the June 1994 *Monthly Labor Review*. A table entitled "Employment Cost Index, wages and salaries by occupation and industry group" shows that civilian workers consisting of private industry, state and local government, but excluding farm, household, and federal government workers, received an average 3.2 percent increase for the twelve months ending in March 1994. White collar workers received an average increase of 3.3 percent for the same time period.

Table 2 shows the percent change in mean salaries for the six positions in each of the last six years. Commenting on the first five of those years in the 1993 report we noted that librarian salaries were increasing at a decreasing rate. That trend has changed in the 1994 report.

Table 2. Percent Change in Mean of Salaries Paid 1988-1994						
Title	88 to 89 %	89 to 90 %	90 to 91 %	91 to 92 %	92 to 93 %	93 to 94 %
Director	+9	+2.0	+8.9	+6.0	+3.9	+4.4
Deputy/Associate/Assistant Director	+14	+3.5	+8.9	+4.0	+0.2	+3.4
Department Head/Branch Head	+12	+4.5	+7.8	+5.7	+0.9	+3.0
Reference/Information Librarian	+9	+6.2	+5.1	+3.2	+1.5	+3.7
Cataloger and/or Classifier	+13	+5.9	+5.2	+2.8	-0.5	+4.1
Children's and/or Young Adult Services Librarian	+15	+6.4	+8.0	+11.3	-2.1	+3.3

SOURCE: ALA SURVEY OF LIBRARIAN SALARIES, 1994

Salaries by Type of Library

When one considers salaries by type of library, it is useful to separate positions into three groups: the administrative positions found in all types of libraries (Director, Deputy/Associate/Assistant Director, Department Head/Branch Head); the other two positions found in all libraries (Reference/Information Librarian, Cataloger and/or Classifier); and the one position found only in public libraries (Children's and/or Young Adult Services Librarian).

The mean of salaries paid is highest in large public libraries for Director and for Deputy/Associate/Assistant Director and lowest for both in four-year colleges. For Department Head/Branch Head, the mean is highest in two-year colleges and lowest in medium-sized public libraries. For the other two common positions, the mean is always highest in two-year colleges and lowest in four-year colleges. For the position found only in public libraries--Children's and/or Young Adult Services Librarian--the mean of salaries paid is higher in large public libraries.

Salaries by Region of the U.S.

In order to determine which region has the highest salaries, we analyzed the six positions and the five library size/type categories. When the region with the highest mean salary was marked for each position in each size/type category, North Atlantic was checked 48 percent of the time, West and Southwest was checked 33 percent of the time, Great Lakes and Plains was highest 18 percent of the time, and Southeast was never highest. This is the second year in a row that West and Southwest has not had the largest percentage of highest mean salaries--a pattern which prevailed in all earlier years of this survey. The lowest mean salary was in the Southeast over 92 percent of the time. This pattern is similar to what has been observed in all previous surveys in this series.

Complicating Factors

When designing this survey over ten years ago, we were aware that several aspects of the patterns of employment in libraries would complicate our efforts. As we talked with respondents and users of the reports over the years, we gained additional insights into several factors which should be taken into consideration when using these results.

The Meaning of "Full-Time"

The questionnaire asked about salaries for **full-time** positions only, but full-time was not defined. There are at least two problems in this area: How many months in a year is full-time? How do you report people who work full-time in the library but part-time at one job and part-time at another?

The months in a year problem primarily affects academic libraries where librarians sometimes have academic year contracts for less than twelve months. In this survey, respondents are asked to indicate the number of months a salary covers and the computer calculated twelve months at the same rate. Appendix G shows how often less-than-twelve-month salaries occur.

Another complication related to the issue of "full-time" is the fact that one librarian may fill more than one position. For example: a public librarian may work part-time as a children's librarian and part-time as a cataloger; an academic librarian may be a reference librarian as well as a department head (of reference department). Survey instructions told the respondent:

> If a staff member works full-time but performs duties of more than one position, list him or her as incumbent in the position which you consider his or her major responsibility. **List each staff member only once.**

The Meaning of "Professional"

In the early years of this survey, respondents were asked to report only salaries paid to professionals, but the word "professional" was not defined. Instead, each position was described in such a way that professional responsibility was clearly implied. Instructions told the respondent to list all incumbents in these positions "regardless of academic credentials." We accepted the judgment of the respondent that the salaries reported were for professional work but found out, when we called about low salaries (see below), that some respondents had doubts about whether a particular incumbent could be described as "professional." When such doubts were expressed, we asked the respondent to make a decision based on the definition in ALA's statement on "Library Education and Personnel Utilization." (See Appendix B, Policy 54.1, Section 8.) In 1990, that definition was added to the instructions.

Beginning with the 1991 survey, we asked respondents to report only staff *with master's degrees from graduate library education programs accredited by ALA*. We know that many respondents paid attention to this instruction because questionnaires were returned to us with notes that no one in the library, or no one in a certain position, had the MLS. On the other hand, we also know that some did not follow instructions because of what we learned when calling about salaries below the cut off point (see below). The questionnaire also requested another type of information which helped to ensure that only salaries for professional positions were included in this report. Following each position title and description was a line for "Position Title (if different from above)." When screening revealed such titles as "secretary," "library assistant" or "technical assistant" on that line, the salary information was not used.

Salaries Below $19,000

In previous years this report has described the methodology used to determine the cut-off point below which salaries were dropped as probably not being for full-time, professional work. The cut-off point for the 1994 survey was $19,000. Of the 11,695 salaries initially entered into the file, thirty-three were below $19,000 (less than 1%). Staff at the Library Research Center conducted telephone interviews with directors at the twenty-two libraries involved and learned that four of the thirty-three salaries were for part-time work or were paid to staff without the specified degree. Those four salaries were dropped from the file used for the report. Once the four salaries were dropped the total was 11,681 salaries. The dropped salaries had been reported primarily because the respondent had misunderstood the instructions. Twenty-nine salaries of less than $19,000 did remain in the file. Twenty-two were in a public library and seven were in an academic library.

Job Levels or Faculty Ranks

The wording of this questionnaire is based on an assumption that librarians are compensated at a particular amount for doing a particular job (e.g., reference). However, in many libraries that is not true. Some libraries use a system of levels in their compensation structure (e.g., Librarian I, II, III, IV) to account for the background a person brings to a job and the amount of responsibility it entails. Compensation is based on level, not on the type of work done as defined by our position descriptions. Some academic libraries pay salaries based on faculty rank rather than work done. In many academic libraries where librarians have faculty rank and titles, they are compensated as Instructor, Assistant Professor, Associate Professor or Professor and not as any one of the position titles on our questionnaire. We do not attempt to account for this variety within the structure of our questionnaire and every year some respondents tell us it was impossible to complete the questionnaire for this reason.

Several respondents and reviewers of this report have recommended in the past that we collect salary data for librarian levels or ranks. We have considered this seriously, but concluded that it would be at least as confusing as the current method due to the fact that levels and ranks mean different things in different libraries.

Longevity Pay

Some large public libraries were unable to report exact salaries for each position due to the large number of incumbents and the small amount of time available. In several such cases, respondents reported the number of incumbents for a position that were in a specific range on the salary schedule and we used the midpoint of that range for the appropriate number of incumbents. While reasonable in a national study that reports summary statistics, this procedure does not take into account longevity pay which is related to individual tenure and not to a point on the salary schedule. Thus some incumbents may be earning more than is reported here.

Level of Experience

Respondents occasionally ask us to ask for and report salaries in a way that takes into account the years of experience that an incumbent possesses. Unfortunately, providing that information would be a burden on respondents and reporting it would make this report overly complex. This report does take such factors into account in two ways: beginning librarian salaries are reported in a separate table and are not included in salary data for specific positions; and data for specific positions show figures at the first and third quartile as well as the mean, median, and range.

Appendix A

Salary Surveys Providing Information on Library Workers

Most library salary surveys listed below are conducted on a regular schedule (annual or biennial) and on a regional or national basis. The library literature should be monitored for reports of one-time surveys by individual libraries or associations. Some state library agencies collect salary and benefits data as part of their ongoing statistical gathering efforts from libraries within their own state. There is wide variation, however, in what data are collected and how these are compiled and reported. Most collect only public library data. Academic and school library data may be collected by other state agencies.

In addition, some state library associations collect salary data, issue recommended salary guidelines, set minimum salaries for professional positions, or publish reports in association journals or newsletters. As of June 1994, nineteen states had established recommended minimum salaries. These include: Connecticut, Delaware, Illinois, Indiana, Iowa, Louisiana, Maine, Massachusetts, New Jersey, North Carolina, Ohio, Pennsylvania, Rhode Island, South Carolina, South Dakota, Texas, Vermont, West Virginia, and Wisconsin. Specific amounts are not listed here because these are regularly updated by the associations. The latest figures can be found in the most recent classified section of *American Libraries* or *College & Research Libraries News*. A list of state library agency and association addresses can be found in *The Bowker Annual: Library and Book Trade Almanac*.

Individual libraries will sometimes conduct private surveys of institutions of comparable size or in the same geographical area, either through an outside consulting firm or by calling libraries informally. For the most part, these surveys are not published, although the initiating library will often share results with participating libraries. Some library workers are also conducting surveys that compare their salaries with other professions and occupations within their jurisdiction in an effort to achieve pay equity with positions requiring comparable skills, effort, responsibilities and working conditions.

Academic Libraries

Association of Research Libraries. *ARL Annual Salary Survey.* Washington, D.C.: ARL.

The annual survey shows the number of filled positions, average years of experience, and average, median and beginning salaries for professional positions in all ARL libraries. In addition, tables present the number of staff, average salaries, and years of experience for 27 position categories and display findings on the present incumbents of these positions by sex and minority group membership, and by geographical location, size, and type of institution. Salaries for staff in law and medical libraries are presented in two separate series of tables. Salary data for staff in Canadian university libraries are also displayed in Canadian dollars.

Order from ARL, 21 DuPont Circle, NW, Suite 800, Washington, D.C. 20036, 202/296-2296. The 1994 survey, published in January 1995, is available for $20/ARL members or $60/nonmembers.

College and University Personnel Association. *1993-94 Administrative CompensationSurvey Report.* Washington, D.C.: CUPA.

Annual survey. 1993-94 survey includes data on 171 college and university administrative positions from 1,417 public and private institutions. The tables in the survey present the median salary and salary percentiles according to institutional budget, enrollment and classification. Directors of library services are included, as well as circulation, acquisitions, reference, technical and public services librarians.

The survey is available from CUPA, 1233 20th St., NW, Suite 503, Washington, D.C. 20036, 202/429-0311; $75 for association members, $175 for non-members/survey participants and $295 for non-members/survey non-participants.

American Library Association. Association of College and Research Libraries. New England Chapter. *Salary Survey of New England College Libraries.*

The New England Chapter publishes this biennial survey, begun in 1986-87. Included are four year undergraduate institutions in the six New England states. Overall average, median and beginning salaries are given for individual institutions and average salaries are given for 24 positions and by size of institution for 4 categories of staff. 1991-92 edition $10. Make check payable to ACRL/NEC Chapter. Contact Fay Zipkowitz, Associate Professor, GSLIS, University of Rhode Island, Kingston, RI 02881 or Christina Bellinger, Dimond Library, University of New Hampshire, Durham, NH 03824.

Public Libraries

American Library Association. Public Library Association. *Public Library Data Service Statistical Report.* Chicago: PLA.

Annual listing with information that includes library-specific salaries for directors and beginning librarians for most public libraries serving 100,000 or more and for many smaller libraries, as well as basic library statistics. The 1994 edition is available from ALA Customer Services Dept., 155 N. Wacker Dr., Chicago, IL 60606-1719, 800/545-2433, press 7. The price is $60 with the usual discounts for PLA and ALA members.

Evelina Moulder. "Salaries of Municipal Officials for 1993" in *The Municipal Year Book 1994.* Washington, D.C.: International City/County Management Association.

Chief librarian salaries for local public libraries are included with earnings of other city department heads. These are reported by geographic region, population size, city type (i.e., central, suburban, independent) and form of government. The mean, median, and first and third quartiles are included for libraries serving ten different population groups ranging from under 2,500 to over 1,000,000. *The Municipal Year Book* is published in April of each year and includes salary data for previous year. For details, contact Evelina Moulder, ICMA, 777 N. Capitol St., Suite 500, Washington, D.C. 20002, 202/962-3651.

A summary table of 1993 salaries from The *Municipal Year Book* is published in *Library Personnel News* 8 (May/June 1994): 5.

Sandstedt, Carl R. *Salary Survey: West-North-Central States*. St. Peters, Mo.: St. Charles City-County Library.

Annual survey provides data for directors, assistant directors, department heads, starting MLS, and several support positions for public libraries in West-North-Central States (North Dakota, South Dakota, Nebraska, Kansas, Minnesota, Iowa, Missouri). Average salaries are presented by size of library budget. Also includes per FTE costs, per capita support, per capita materials budget.

Usually available in April for current calendar year. Send $5.00 for first copy, $2.00 per additional copy. Diskettes with .WKS files are $10. Please prepay. A $5 invoicing fee will be made for all orders requiring an invoice. Contact Salary Survey, St. Charles City-County Library, 425 Spencer Rd., Box 529, St. Peters, MO 63376, 314/441-2300.

School Libraries

Educational Research Service, Inc. *National Survey of Salaries and Wages in Public Schools*. Arlington, Va.: ERS.

Since 1974-75, ERS has published an annual report of salaries for public school personnel, which includes data for school librarians and library clerks. Usually published in three volumes, the report covers scheduled salaries for professional personnel and actual salaries paid for professional and support personnel by enrollment group, per pupil expenditure, and geographic region.

The 1993-94 report costs $54 for each of the three volumes; available from ERS, 2000 Clarendon Blvd., Arlington, VA 22201, 703/243-2100.

Miller, Marilyn L., and Schontz, Marilyn. "Expenditures for Resources in School Library Media Centers," *School Library Journal*.

As part of a report every two years on budgets for and expenditures by school library media centers, some median and mean salary data for media specialists are reported by level of school. Included are comparisons of schools with and without district level library media coordinators. October 1993 issue has the latest data.

National Education Association. *Estimates of School Statistics*. Washington, D.C.: NEA.

Annual statistical data for the 50 states and District of Columbia includes estimated average annual salaries of total instructional staff and also separate data for classroom teachers by state and region. Librarian data are not given separately, however, but are grouped with teachers, principals, supervisors, guidance and psychological personnel and related instructional workers.

The annual compilation is usually available each spring. The 1992-93 report, published in 1993, is available for $14.95 for non-NEA members. Contact NEA Professional Library, PO Box 509, West Haven, CT 06516, 203/934-2669, 800-229-4200.

Law Libraries

American Association of Law Libraries. *1993 Salary Survey.* Revised edition. Chicago: AALL, 1993.

Results of a survey of AALL members provides salary data as of April 1993 by type of law library, gender, position, years of experience, geographic area, and educational degree. Available for $50 from AALL, 53 W. Jackson Blvd., Suite 940, Chicago, IL 60604, 312/939-4764.

American Association of Law Libraries. *Survey of Private Law Libraries.* Chicago: AALL in cooperation with SLA.

The survey provides compensation data for a variety of administrative and support staff positions and by functional areas, years of experience, budget range, and number of patrons served. Compensation is defined as salary as well as any cash bonuses received.

The 1991 survey report is the latest report available for $70 from AALL, 53 W. Jackson Blvd., Suite 940, Chicago, IL 60604, 312/939-4764.

American Bar Association. *Comprehensive Law Library Statistical Table.* Office of Consultant on Legal Education.

Annual survey based on questionnaire by the American Bar Association to 176 law school libraries. Salary data are a small part of other statistics gathered. Includes median and average salaries of full time professional law librarians and support staff by school. Full report for $125 from the Assistant Consultant on Legal Education to the American Bar Association, c/o James P. White, Indiana University, 550 W. North Street, Indianapolis, IN 46202, 317/264-8340.

Malmquist, Katherine E. "Academic Law Librarians Today: Survey of Salary and Position Information." *Law Library Journal* 85 (Winter 1993): 135-183.

Results of 1991 survey of 111 academic law libraries are reported with low, median and high salaries for fifteen positions, five regions and by gender and library size.

Other Special Libraries

Art Libraries Society of North America. *ARLIS/NA Salary Survey, 1990.* Tucson, Ariz.: ARLIS/NA, 1991.

Latest salary survey of ARLIS/NA members provides information separately for those who spend 50 percent or more of their time with visual resources (e.g., slides, photographs, film, video) and those who work primarily with textual materials. Data were analyzed in relation to several variables (region, type of parent institution, library degree and arts degree). Full, 32-page report available for $10 prepaid from ARLIS/NA, 3900 E. Timrod St., Tucson, AZ 85711, 602/881-8479. Summary report in *Art Documentation* 11:93-94 (Summer 1992).

Association of Academic Health Sciences Library Directors. *Annual Statistics of Medical School Libraries in the United States and Canada.* Seattle, Washington.

Salaries are provided for director, associate director, division head, department head, other librarians, and entry level positions. Minimum, maximum and mean are provided for the positions and arranged by region.

Salary data for 1993-94 are included in the 16th edition. It is available at a cost of $50 for members of the Association of Academic Health Sciences Library Directors and $100 for nonmembers. This edition and previous editions may be ordered by contacting AAHSLD, 2033 Sixth Ave., #804, Seattle, WA 98121, 206/441-6020.

Medical Library Association. *MLA Salary Survey.* Chicago: MLA.

Triennial survey data cover geographic area, position level, type of institution, years of experience, education, primary area of responsibility, benefits, and other information.

The 1992 MLA member salary survey is available at a cost of $26.00 for members; $52.00 for nonmembers from MLA, 6 N. Michigan Ave., Suite 300, Chicago, IL 60602, 312/419-9094.

Special Libraries Association. *SLA Biennial Salary Survey.* Washington, D.C.: SLA.

Since 1967, SLA conducted an in-depth salary survey of members every three years. As of 1990, the in-depth survey is conducted every two years. Results are now issued as separate publications. Salaries are reported at the 25th, 50th (median) and 75th percentiles and contain breakdowns by industry, geographic region, administrative responsibility, sex, education level, and experience. Data for the U.S. and Canada are presented in separate tables. Annual updates, using a random sampling of 25 percent of the membership and an abbreviated questionnaire, were started in 1977 and are used in years between the now biennial surveys. The results of the updates are published in *Special Libraries* in the fall issue.

The survey data collected in 1992 were published in 1993; the report sells for $30 (members); $37.50 (non-members). Data collected in 1994 will be published in late 1994. Contact Special Libraries Association, 1700 18th St., N.W., Washington, D.C. 20009, 202/234-4700.

State Library Agencies

Chief Officers of State Library Agencies. "COSLA--Table 1 - Salary Data: State Library Agencies." Lexington, Ky.

The annual survey of salary data for state library agencies compiled earlier by the Association of Specialized and Cooperative Library Agencies now is carried out by the Chief Officers of State Library Agencies (COSLA). Included is information on the salary for each state for a variety of positions: state librarian, assistant director, director of library operations or library services, director of library development or networking, FSCS data coordinator, consultants, specialists, and beginning professionals.

To order, contact Angela Crouch, COSLA Office, 167 W. Main St., Suite 600, Lexington, KY 40507, 606/231-1925.

Other

Association for Library and Information Science Education. *Library and Information Science Education Statistical Report*. Raleigh, NC.: ALISE, 1980-.

Average and median salaries for faculty and administrators in ALISE member schools are provided in this annual report by sex, rank and term of appointment.

Back issues (1981-) of the report are available from ALISE, 4101 Lake Boone Trail, Suite 201, Raleigh, NC 27607, 919/787-5181 for $15 each plus postage and handling: $4.00. Current issue is $30.00 plus postage and handling (U.S. funds). Annual report usually published in the summer.

College and University Personnel Association. *1993-94 National Faculty Salary Survey by Discipline and Rank in Public Colleges and Universities*. Washington, D.C.: CUPA.

College and University Personnel Association. *1993-94 National Faculty Salary Survey by Discipline and Rank in Private Colleges and Universities*. Washington, D.C.: CUPA.

Annual surveys collect data for five faculty ranks in 55 disciplines and major fields. A total 307 public and 490 private institutions participated in the most recent study. Communications, Communication Technologies, Computer Information Sciences, and Library and Archival Sciences are included. The listings are for those who teach in library science programs, not those who hold faculty rank as academic librarians. Faculty Salary Surveys are each $30 for survey participants, $50 for CUPA members/survey non-participants and $75 for non-members/survey non-participants from CUPA, 1233 20th St., NW, Suite 301, Washington, D.C. 20036, 202/429-0311.

Martinez, Ed and Raymond Roney. "1993 Library Support Staff Salary Survey." *Library Mosaics*, May/June 1994, pp. 6-10.

Reports salaries as of fall 1993 by type of library (public, special, academic), four regions of the U.S. and the staff classifications of clerk, assistant, technician, and other non master's degree positions.

Zipkowitz, Fay. "Placements and Salaries." *Library Journal*. Annual.

Annual survey since 1951 of recent graduates of ALA-accredited library education programs (usually published in a fall issue of *Library Journal* with data from previous calendar year.) For each reporting school, the low, high, average and median salaries are reported for men, women, and total placements. This information is also provided for five regions of the U.S. An additional table shows the distribution of high, low, average and median salaries by type of library for men, women and total placements. The latest listing, "Placements and Salaries 1992" was published in *Library Journal*, October 15, 1993 (pp. 30-36). Canadian schools are no longer included.

Employee Benefits

Although some states collect data on employee benefits, little information is collected on a regional or national level on a regular basis for library workers.

American Library Association. Office for Library Personnel Resources. "Library Employee Benefits." Chicago. ALA, 1991.

Results of informal survey of public and academic library personnel directors and administrators regarding employee benefits. Summary report in *Library Personnel News*, vol. 5, no. 4, July-August 1991.

Association of Research Libraries. Office of Management Services. *Benefits for Professional Staff in ARL Libraries*. SPEC Kit 197. Washington, D.C.: ARL, 1993.

Results of a survey of benefits provided by ARL member institutions in 1993 are reported. Information on availability of health care and life insurance, retirement benefits, leave policies, and other perequisites are summarized. Sample policies from ARL libraries are included. Order for $45.50 from ARL, 21 DuPont Circle NW, Washington, DC 20036, 202/296-8656.

PROVIDENCE Associates, Inc. *Public Library Work Benefits Survey*. Denton, Texas: 1994.

Results of a survey of 75 public libraries in 1994 provides salary ranges and average salaries for 5 staff levels, plus data on vacation days, holidays, sick leave, leave of absence, pension plans, health and life insurance, and other benefits. Single copies available for $27.50 plus $2.50 postage/handling, from PROVIDENCE Associates, Inc., 419 S. Carroll Blvd. 2A, Denton, TX 76201-5928, 817/566-0417.

Salary Surveys for Other Library Workers and Related Information Professionals

For salary data on other types of workers that may be employed in libraries, the following surveys might be useful:

Abbott, Langer and Associates, 548 First St., Crete, IL 60417.

Conducts annual salary surveys for the following fields: legal and related jobs in business and industry; industrial engineers; plant engineers; consulting engineering firms; service department; nonprofit organizations; research and development; manufacturing; security/loss prevention; MIS/data processing; accounting/financial jobs; sales/marketing management; personnel/industrial relations; and inter-city wage and salary differentials.

The *Compensation in Nonprofit Organizations* report contains information on salaries of Directors of Information with this type of employer. Mean, median, 1st & 3rd quartile, and 1st & 9th decile data, salary ranges, current salaries, and total compensation (salaries plus bonuses) are reported by supervisory responsibility, type of nonprofit organization, total annual budget, geographic scope of organization, number of employees, region, state, and metropolitan area.

Annotations of over 1,200 salary surveys, both domestic and foreign, can be found in *Available Pay Survey Reports: An Annotated Bibliography* (4th ed.) by Dr. Steven Langer (1994). Annotations are indexed by source, geographic area, type of employer, and job title/function/college curricula.

The AMS Foundation, 550 W. Jackson Blvd., Ste. 360, Chicago, IL 60661, 312/236-1840.

Conducts annual surveys of clerical, professional, data processing and middle management jobs as well as pertinent business trends. The *Office Secretarial, Professional, Data Processing and Management Survey* sells for $350; *Contract Labor, Flexible Work, Business Expenses and New Benefits* sell for $30 each.

Datamation publishes an annual salary survey of computer and information systems personnel. The 1994 report will be in the October 15, 1994 issue. This reports on average salaries for positions in systems analysis, programming, database administration, data entry, office automation, and computer operations, by industry and regions.

The *Public Relations Journal* publishes an annual survey of public relations personnel in its July issue.

U.S. Department of Labor, Bureau of Labor Statistics *Area Wage Surveys*.

The Bureau also publishes annual surveys of professional, administrative, technical and clerical positions. Primary fields covered are accounting, law, personnel management, engineering, chemistry, retail, clerical supervisory, drafting and clerical. These surveys may provide useful data on non-librarian professional or specialist positions and on clerical positions. A subject bibliography on "Prices, Wages, and the Cost of Living" (SB.226) is available from GPO and gives order information for the area wage surveys and other publications on compensation.

Each year surveys are done in over seventy standard metropolitan areas. The surveys concentrate on clerical and manual labor occupations; however, these will be useful as a source of pay data for clerical positions. Specifies average workweek and mean, median, and middle pay rates, as well as vacation benefits, insurance and pension plans, and shift differential information.

Appendix B

ALA Policies Relating to Salary Issues

The following are policies endorsed by the ALA Council and included in the "ALA Policy Manual" which appears annually in the *ALA Handbook of Organization*.

Policy #54.1 Library Education and Personnel Utilization

Sec. 8 The title "Librarian" carries with it the connotation of "professional" in the sense that professional tasks are those which require a special background and education on the basis of which library needs are identified, problems are analyzed, goals are set, and original and creative solutions are formulated for them, integrating theory into practice, and planning, organizing, communicating, and administering successful programs of service to users of the library's materials and services. In defining services to users, the professional person recognizes potential users as well as current ones, and designs services which will reach all who could benefit from them.

Sec. 9 The title "Librarian" therefore should be used only to designate positions in libraries which utilize the qualifications and impose the responsibilities suggested above. Positions which are primarily devoted to the routine application of established rules and techniques, however useful and essential to the effective operation of a library's ongoing services, should not carry the word "Librarian" in the job title.

Sec. 11 The salaries for each (personnel) category should offer a range of promotional steps sufficient to permit a career-in-rank. The top salary in any category should overlap the beginning salary in the next higher category, in order to give recognition to the value of experience and knowledge gained on the job.

Sec. 19 Administrative responsibilities entail advanced knowledge and skills comparable to those represented by any other high-level specialty, and appointment to positions in top administration should normally require the qualifications of a Senior Librarian with a specialization in administration. This category, however, is not limited to administrators, whose specialty is only one of several specializations of value to the library service. There are many areas of special knowledge within librarianship which are equally important and to which equal recognition in prestige and salary should be given. Highly qualified persons with specialist responsibilities in some aspects of librarianship--archives, bibliography, reference, for example--should be eligible for advanced status and financial rewards without being forced to abandon for administrative responsibilities their areas of major competence.

Policy #54.4 Comparable Rewards

The American Library Association supports salary administration which gives reasonable and comparable recognition to positions having administrative, technical, subject, and linguistic requirements. It is recognized that all such specialist competencies can be intellectually vigorous and meet demanding professional operational needs. In administering such a policy, it can be a useful guide that, in major libraries, as many nonadministrative specialities be assigned to the top classifications as are administrative staff. Whenever possible there should be as many at the top rank with less than 30 percent administrative load as there are at the highest rank carrying over 70 percent administrative load.

Policy #54.7 Security of Employment for Library Employees

Security of employment, as an elementary right, guarantees specifically......a sufficient degree of economic security to make employment in the library attractive to men and women of ability.

Policy #54.8 The Library's Pay Plan

Libraries should have a well-constructed and well-administered pay plan based on systematic analysis and evaluation of jobs in the library and which will assure equal pay for equal work. (Note: For text of full statement, see section following listing of policies.)

Policy #54.9 Permanent Part-Time Employment

The right to earn a living includes a right to part-time employment on a par with full-time employment, including prorated pay and fringe benefits, opportunity for advancement and protection of tenure, access to middle and upper level jobs, and exercise of full responsibilities at any level.

ALA shall create more voluntarily chosen upgraded permanent part-time jobs in its own organization and supports similar action on the part of all libraries.

Policy #54.10 Equal Opportunity and Salaries

The American Library Association supports and works for the achievement of equal salaries and opportunity for employment and promotion for men and women.

The Association fully supports the concept of comparable wages for comparable work that aims at levels of pay for female-oriented occupations equal to those of male-oriented occupations; ALA therefore supports all legal and legislative efforts to achieve wages for library workers commensurate with wages in other occupations with similar qualifications, training, and responsibilities.

ALA particularly supports the efforts of those library workers who have documented, and are legally challenging, the practice of discriminatory salaries, and whose success will benefit all library workers throughout the nation.

Policy #54.11 Collective Bargaining

The American Library Association recognizes the principle of collective bargaining as one of the methods of conducting labor-management relations used by private and public institutions. The Association affirms the right of eligible library employees to organize and bargain collectively with their employees, or to refrain from organizing and bargaining collectively, without fear of reprisal.

Policy #54.18 Advertising Salary Ranges

Available ranges shall be given for positions listed in any placement services provided by ALA and its units. A regional salary guide delineating the latest minimum salary figures recommended by state library associations shall be made available from any placement services provided by ALA and its units.

All ALA and unit publications printing classified job advertisements shall list all available salary ranges established for open positions and shall include a regional salary guide delineating the latest minimum salary figures recommended by state library associations for library positions.

Full Text of Policy # 54.8: The Library's Pay Plan*

The American Library Association believes that an important factor in establishing and maintaining good library service is adequate pay for library employees as exemplified in a well-constructed and well-administered pay plan. A knowledge of the principles on which sound salary administration is based must be the foundation of an equitable pay plan. To aid the library's governing board, its administration, and its staff in the formulation, promulgation, and operation of such a pay plan, the ALA Board on Personnel Administration sets forth in a series of related statements the principles of salary planning and administration.

1. A sound pay plan will be predicated on a systematic analysis and evaluation of jobs in the library, and will reflect the current organization and objectives of the library, recognizing different levels of difficulty and responsibility inherent in various positions, whether these are classifed as professional, nonprofessional, administrative, specialist, maintenance, or trade; the relationship among positions in terms of difficulty and responsibility will thus be expressed in a unified plan which will integrate all types of service and will assure equal pay for equal work.

2. An equitable salary schedule will be provided for each class of position which is comparable to that received by persons employed in analogous work in the area and required to have analogous training and qualifications.

    The salaries of nonprofessional employees, maintenance and skilled trade workers employed by the library system will compare with those of local workers performing similar duties. The salary schedules for professional library positions, in the case of the community where the pay scale does not meet competing rates outside, may need to exceed the prevailing local level for other professional personnel. Since the recruiting of professionally trained librarians is on a nation-wide basis, the library system must compete with rates paid in the country as a whole in order to obtain and retain a high quality of professional personnel. In libraries in educational institutions (elementary, secondary, and higher education) the professional librarians will normally be on the faculty pay plan, with the salary schedules of the various classes of faculty rank adjusted to compensate equitably for such factors as shorter vacations and longer work week; where a separate pay plan is used, it will be comparable with that of the faculty and adjusted to compensate equitably for such factors as vacation and work week.

3. An equitable salary schedule will provide for each class of position a minimum and a maximum salary and a series of increments within each salary range, such increments to be granted on the basis of demonstrated competence, individual development (whether through growth on the job or through formal education), and attitude.

---

*Note: This policy was passed by the ALA Council in July 1955. It still remains a useful statement regarding the administration of a library's pay plan. Readers should note, however, that the references to the Board on Personnel Administration are not applicable since this unit is no longer in existence.

4. The library system in developing a pay plan, and in reviewing it to maintain its adequacy, will identify one or more key positions in the professional and in the other services, set salary schedules for these positions which are comparable to prevailing rates for such positions, and develop and adjust the salary schedule for other levels of positions in relation to the salary schedules set for each of these key positions.

5. The pay plan ladder consisting of the salary schedules for the various classes of positions will provide an orderly progression from the lowest to the highest schedule, with each schedule reflecting properly the difference in level of duties and responsibilities of positions in that classification from those in the schedule below and above it but without wide gaps or serious overlapping between schedules.

6. An equitable pay plan will reflect living costs in the community, the cost of maintaining an appropriate level of living, and the ability of the jurisdiction to pay for the service.

7. All policies and rules concerning the operation and administration of the pay plan will be set forth clearly in writing and will accompany the pay plan.

8. Though final approval and adoption of the pay plan and rules for its operation rest with the governing board and administration of the library, it is desirable that the library staff participates in the formulation of both the plan and its operating rules.

9. Each staff member will be informed of the salary schedule for his or her class of position, of the relation of that schedule to the pay plan as a whole, and of the policies and rules governing the operation of the plan.

Appendix C

Selected Bibliography on Compensation and Employee Benefits

Compiled by the
ALA Office for Library Personnel Resources

Note: The earlier editions of **ALA Survey of Librarian Salaries** contained selected citations on compensation that readers may wish to consult since many of these references are still useful. Items listed below have been published since the previous listings were compiled.

American Library Association Committee on Pay Equity. *Pay Equity: A Matter of Fairness.* Video produced by James Comes (18 min.) Chicago: ALA Office for Library Personnel Resources, 1994.

American Library Association Committee on Pay Equity. "Raising Library Salaries: What Library Trustees Can Do." (Brochure). Chicago: ALA, 1994.

American Library Association Committee on Pay Equity. "Raising Library Salaries: What Library Workers Can Do." (Brochure). Chicago: ALA, 1994.

Fuehrer, Vicki. "Total Reward Strategy: A Prescription for Organizational Survival." *Compensation and Benefits Review* 26: 44-53 (January-February 1994).

Hogarty, Donna Brown. "New Ways to Pay." *Management Review* 83: 34-36 (January 1994).

Haslinger, John A. and Donna Sheerin. "Employee Input: The Key to Successful Benefits Programs." *Compensation and Benefits Review* 26: 61-70 (May-June 1994).

Johnson, Bradford A. and Harry H. Ray. "Employee-Developed Pay Systems Increasing Productivity." *Personnel Journal* 72: 112-115+ (November 1993).

Kohn, Alfie. "Why Incentive Plans Cannot Work." *Harvard Business Review* 71: 54-63 (September-October 1993).

LeBlanc, Peter V. and Michael McInerney. "Need a Change? Jump on the Banding Wagon." *Personnel Journal* 73: 72-78 (January 1994).

National Committee on Pay Equity. *Erase the Bias: A Pay Equity Guide to Eliminating Race and Sex Bias.* Washington, D.C.: NCPE, 1993.

O'Neill, Graham L. and Deirdre Lander. "Linking Employee Skills to Pay: A Framework for Skill-Based Pay Plans." *ACA Journal* (American Compensation Association) 2: 14-27 (Winter 1993-1994).

Poole, Jeanne C., William F. Rathgeber III, and Stanley W. Silverman. "Paying for Performance in a TQM Environment." *HRMagazine* 38: 68-74 (October 1993).

Risher, Howard and Robert J. Butler. "Salary Banding: An Alternative Salary-Management Concept." *ACA Journal* (American Compensation Association) 2: 48-57 (Winter 1993-1994).

Smeenk, Brian P. "Canada's Pay Equity Experiments." *HRMagazine* 38: 58-61 (September 1993).

Woika, Michael. "Pay Plan Based on Performance Motivates Employees." *HRMagazine* 38: 68-74 (October 1993).

Zipkowitz, Fay. "Fewer Graduates but Salaries Climb." *Library Journal* 118: 30-36 (October 15, 1993).

Appendix D

Technical Considerations

Formation of Library Groups

As in previous years, the survey samples were selected from two library universes--public and academic. The public library universe included all public libraries serving populations of 25,000 or more and was stratified into two classes--those serving populations of from 25,000 to 99,999 and those serving populations of 100,000 or more.

The academic library universe was stratified into three classes: two-year college, four-year college, and university. This stratification was based on the "Highest Offering" code used in the *1994 Higher Education Directory* published by Higher Education Publications, Inc. The first of these three classes include schools that offer "two but less than four years." The second includes schools that offer a "four or five year baccalaureate." The third combines four categories: "first professional degree," "master's," "beyond master's but less than doctorate," "doctorate."

Within each of these five strata, libraries were further stratified into four geographic areas used frequently by National Center for Education Statistics (NCES): North Atlantic, Great Lakes and Plains, Southeast, and West and Southwest. A list of states included in each region is provided in Table D-1. As in previous surveys, the five library classes and four geographic areas were combined to form twenty groups from which samples were selected. Tables D2-D7 show the size of each group, the size of the sample, and the size of the return.

Sample Selection and Return

The size of the sample for each type/size/geographic strata was determined by using a proportional sampling procedure that took into account the size of the population in each group and the expected return rate for the survey. As has been done since 1992, the public library sample was selected using a diskette from the NCES containing data on all public libraries submitted to NCES by state library agencies as part of the Federal State Cooperative System for Public Library Data (FSCS). This file includes data on the number of staff with master's degrees from graduate library education programs accredited by ALA. Before selecting the sample, we dropped from the sampling frame libraries that did not have at least two of such personnel. Once the sampling frame was established, the sample was drawn by strata as described above.

The procedure for selecting the academic library sample was the same as the procedure followed in 1993. We obtained a customized sampling frame from John Minter Associates based on the *1994 Higher Education Directory* and a tape from NCES on "Academic Libraries, 1990." Minter screened out several sets of institutions from the full universe. Removed were institutions with fewer than two full-time professionals and institutions categorized as "specialized" by the Carnegie Corporation for the Advancement of Teaching. Those institutions offer degrees ranging from the bachelor's to the doctorate, at least 50 percent of which are in a single specialized field, e.g., "theological seminaries, Bible colleges, and other institutions offering degrees in religion," and "Schools of art, music, and design." Specialized institutions often declined to respond in the early years of this survey. Also excluded were four sets of institutions whose individual members had been unable to respond in the past. In New York, the seventeen institutions that are part of the City University of New York were removed because librarians there have full academic status and salary is not related to position description. Public two-year schools in California were removed for the same reason as were the fourteen members of the state university system in Pennsylvania. Also in Pennsylvania, we removed all but the main campus of Pennsylvania State University because librarians at other campuses declined to respond in the past and referred us to the main campus. The remaining institutions were sampled using the stratification plan described above. Finally, the preliminary sample was screened for libraries that refused to respond in the years from 1990 through 1993 for reasons that seemed unlikely to change. Seven such libraries were dropped from the sample.

In addition to the 964 returns analyzed for this report, we also received 26 returns that could not be used. They fell into the following categories:

- nine were simply blank

- three were from respondents in libraries where none of the full-time staff had master's degrees from graduate library education programs accredited by ALA.

- two were refusals. Both were from academic libraries.

- twelve were unusable for miscellaneous reasons (e.g., contributed services staff only, label was removed, reorganization puts in different strata, incomplete data).

Procedure

The questionnaire and cover letter were mailed on March 31, 1994. A postage-paid business reply envelope was enclosed to encourage response. A second mailing was sent to all non-respondents in April. A third mailing was sent in May only to non-respondents in several strata where response was under 70 percent.

After questionnaires were screened at ALA, they were sent to the Library Research Center (LRC) of the University of Illinois Graduate School of Library and Information Science, where they were edited, entered into a microcomputer file, and analyzed using SPSS/PC+ (the microcomputer version of the Statistical Package for the Social Sciences).

Again this year a special procedure was followed for libraries that are members of the Association of Research Libraries. ARL, which includes about 100 of the largest university libraries in the U.S., conducts its own annual salary survey. Data are gathered for salaries as of July 1 and published the following spring. ARL libraries are also included in the sample for the ALA survey. In the past, some have declined to answer because they are unable to spend time completing another salary questionnaire. For the 1994 survey, ARL again agreed to cooperate with us to save work for everyone. After the sample was selected, we identified the ARL libraries on the list and sent the directors a special mailing asking them to release salaries already on file with ARL. All but three of the thirty-four ARL libraries in the sample agreed to release data. We sent ARL a list of the ARL position codes that matched the position descriptions in our questionnaire and ARL sent us salary data on diskette for those positions in the selected institutions. These salaries were entered into the data file along with salaries from other libraries.

This procedure worked well and saved time both in the libraries involved and in survey processing. It has two drawbacks, however. ARL salary figures are as of July 1993 whereas others are as of the following April. Thus, the figures for salaries in the university category in our report may be lower than what was paid in April 1994. Also, ARL does not specify that salaries should be reported only for staff with master's degrees from graduate library education programs accredited by ALA and ARL does include "other professionals" as well as librarians. For the most part, however, we expect that those "other professionals" are in the ARL position code of "Functional Specialist" which was *not* on the list of codes we requested from ARL. On balance, we believe this procedure had more benefits than drawbacks and intend to continue it as long as ARL is willing to cooperate.

Table D-1. States In Four Regions of the U.S.

NORTH ATLANTIC	GREAT LAKES AND PLAINS	SOUTHEAST	WEST AND SOUTHWEST
Connecticut	Illinois	Alabama	Alaska
Delaware	Indiana	Arkansas	Arizona
District of Columbia	Iowa	Florida	California
Maine	Kansas	Georgia	Colorado
Maryland	Michigan	Kentucky	Hawaii
Massachusetts	Minnesota	Louisiana	Idaho
New Hampshire	Missouri	Mississippi	Montana
New Jersey	Nebraska	North Carolina	Nevada
New York	North Dakota	South Carolina	New Mexico
Pennsylvania	Ohio	Tennessee	Oklahoma
Rhode Island	South Dakota	Virginia	Oregon
Vermont	Wisconsin	West Virginia	Texas
			Utah
			Washington
			Wyoming

Source: *Statistics of Public Libraries, 1977-78* (NCES, 1982)

Table D-2. Medium-Sized Public Libraries: Size of Group, Sample, Return

	GROUP	SAMPLE		RETURN	
	#	#	% of Group	#	% of Sample
North Atlantic	317	117	36.9	88	75.2
Great Lakes & Plains	280	103	36.8	85	82.5
Southeast	166	60	36.1	51	85.0
West and Southwest	178	65	36.5	50	76.9
TOTAL	941	345	36.7	274	79.4

Table D-3. Large Public Libraries: Size of Group, Sample, Return

	GROUP	SAMPLE		RETURN	
	#	#	% of Group	#	% of Sample
North Atlantic	80	46	57.5	31	67.4
Great Lakes & Plains	91	46	50.5	41	89.1
Southeast	129	56	43.4	48	85.7
West and Southwest	138	68	49.3	56	82.4
TOTAL	438	216	49.3	176	81.5

Table D-4. Two-Year College Libraries: Size of Group, Sample, Return

	GROUP	SAMPLE		RETURN	
	#	#	% of Group	#	% of Sample
North Atlantic	117	45	38.5	36	80.0
Great Lakes & Plains	106	45	42.5	33	73.3
Southeast	174	60	34.5	39	65.0
West and Southwest	123	45	36.6	31	68.9
TOTAL	520	195	37.5	139	71.3

Table D-5. Four-Year College Libraries: Size of Group, Sample, Return

	GROUP	SAMPLE		RETURN	
	#	#	% of Group	#	% of Sample
North Atlantic	90	45	50.0	35	77.8
Great Lakes & Plains	115	45	39.1	35	77.8
Southeast	174	45	25.9	30	66.7
West and Southwest	36	33	91.7	26	78.8
TOTAL	415	168	40.5	126	75.0

Table D-6. University Libraries: Size of Group, Sample, Return

	GROUP	SAMPLE		RETURN	
	#	#	% of Group	#	% of Sample
North Atlantic	245	89	36.3	67	75.3
Great Lakes & Plains	226	82	36.3	60	73.2
Southeast	112	74	66.1	62	83.8
West and Southwest	207	76	36.7	60	78.9
TOTAL	790	321	40.6	249	77.6

Table D-7. All Libraries Surveyed: Size of Group, Sample, Return

	GROUP	SAMPLE		RETURN	
	#	#	% of Group	#	% of Sample
North Atlantic	849	342	40.3	257	75.1
Great Lakes & Plains	818	321	39.2	254	79.1
Southeast	755	295	39.1	230	78.0
West and Southwest	682	287	42.1	223	77.7
TOTAL	3,104	1,245	40.1	964	77.4

Appendix E

AMERICAN LIBRARY ASSOCIATION

50 EAST HURON STREET   CHICAGO, ILLINOIS 60611-2795   U.S.A.
312-944-6780   800-545-2433
TELEX: 4909992000 ALA UI   FAX: 312-440-9374   TDD: 312-944-7298

March 31, 1994

Dear Colleague:

ALA needs your help in providing information to the library community. The enclosed survey concerns salaries paid to librarians with master's degrees from programs accredited by ALA who hold full-time positions in academic and public libraries. Your institution has been selected as part of a random sample of libraries to receive the enclosed questionnaire. Only summary results will be reported; individual responses will not be identified.

ALA collected and published similar information biennially from 1982 to 1988, and annually since 1989. The results of these surveys have been useful to many people in the library community who need to know what salary might be paid to someone in a particular type of library position or in a particular geographical area. This information is useful to librarians applying for positions, to librarians setting salaries, and to many others interested in the compensation of librarians.

Because your library is one of a scientifically selected sample, your response is essential to the success of the survey. As an indication of our thanks for your help, all participants are entitled to a 25% discount on the price of the report. (Mention this entitlement when you place an order. The report will be published in September, 1994.) If your staff is very large and this form is difficult to use, please contact Mary Jo Lynch at one of the numbers given below. We want your response and will work with you to make use of whatever data you can provide.

Please complete the questionnaire and return it in the enclosed self-addressed, postage-paid envelope. Please return it as soon as possible, but no later than **April 18, 1994**. If you have questions about the survey, please contact Mary Jo Lynch, Director, ALA Office for Research and Statistics at 1-800-545-2433, extension 4273; Mary.Jo.Lynch@ALA.Org (Internet); or UØ8774@UICVM (Bitnet).

Sincerely yours,

Peggy Sullivan
Executive Director
American Library Association

PS/srg

Enclosures (2)

P.S. Please help our budget by returning this form promptly. In order to ensure the validity of the results, reminders will be sent to nonrespondents. However, we would rather spend the postage money on other services.

Appendix F

AMERICAN LIBRARY ASSOCIATION SURVEY OF LIBRARIAN SALARIES, 1994

PART I. SALARIES PAID TO BEGINNING LIBRARIANS

A. Within the last 12 months has the library hired any full-time staff with master's degrees from graduate library education programs accredited by ALA but no professional experience? Circle one

No (if so, skip to Part II) 1
Yes 2

B. What is the annual salary paid such staff? Please list all annual salaries below as of April 1, 1994. **Do not repeat salaries of these librarians in Part II.** NOTE FOR ACADEMIC LIBRARIES: If the incumbent works LESS than a 12-month year (including vacation), please report the salary and circle the appropriate number of months (9 or 10) for which the salary is paid.

Annual Salary	Annual Salary	Annual Salary	Annual Salary
1 _____ 9 10	3 _____ 9 10	5 _____ 9 10	7 _____ 9 10
2 _____ 9 10	4 _____ 9 10	6 _____ 9 10	8 _____ 9 10

PART II. SALARIES PAID TO LIBRARIANS IN SELECTED POSITIONS

This section of the questionnaire requests information on annual salaries for selected positions ordinarily held by full-time staff with master's degrees from graduate library education programs accredited by ALA.

We realize that many libraries have positions that are not included in the questionnaire. **Do not include salaries for those positions.** Libraries may also fill the positions listed here with staff who have credentials other than master's degrees from graduate library education programs accredited by ALA. **Do not include salaries for those staff. Also, do not include salaries for part-time or support staff.**

Each page in Part II contains descriptions of several specific library positions. If your library has one or more staff with the specified degree employed **FULL-TIME** whose major responsibilities are covered by the position description, please provide the information requested on the form unless the salary was listed above in Part I, B. If a staff member works full-time but performs duties of more than one position, list him or her as incumbent in the position that you consider his or her major responsibility. **List each staff member only once** and give the full salary paid to the person. All **FULL-TIME** incumbents in these positions should be included regardless of the number of months worked in a year.* NOTE FOR ACADEMIC LIBRARIES: If the incumbent is considered full-time but works LESS than a 12-month year (including vacation), please report the salary and circle the appropriate number of months (9 or 10) for which the salary is paid.

For each position in which you have staff with master's degrees from graduate library education programs accredited by ALA employed **FULL-TIME**, please provide the annual salary of each incumbent as of April 1, 1994 except for the beginning librarians reported in Part I, B. Give actual dollars paid. Do not include fringe benefits. If you need additional space, please use separate sheets of paper or attach a computer printout.

*If services are contributed (i.e., institution pays some expenses or an honorarium but not a true salary), please do not list the incumbent.

POSITION TITLE: *Director* *

POSITION DESCRIPTION: Chief administrative officer of the library or library system. Plans and directs all aspects of the operation. May have job title such as Librarian or Head Librarian.

POSITION TITLE: *(if different from above)* _____

ANNUAL SALARY _____ 9 10

Note for academic libraries: Circle 9 or 10 as appropriate if salary is for LESS than a 12 month year (including vacation).

POSITION TITLE: *Deputy/Associate/Assistant Director* *

POSITION DESCRIPTION: Aids Director in planning and directing some or all aspects of library or library system. May manage a major aspect of the library operation (e.g., technical services, public services, collection development, systems/automation).

POSITION TITLE: *(if different from above)* _____

Annual Salary	Annual Salary	Annual Salary	Annual Salary
1 _____ 9/10	3 _____ 9/10	5 _____ 9/10	7 _____ 9/10
2 _____ 9/10	4 _____ 9/10	6 _____ 9/10	8 _____ 9/10

POSITION TITLE: *Department Head/Branch Head* *

POSITION DESCRIPTION: Manages operation of a library unit that is physically separate from the main library (e.g., a branch or a department library) or of one aspect of the main library (e.g., Reference Department, Serials Department, Children's Department).

POSITION TITLE: *(if different from above)* _____

Annual Salary	Annual Salary	Annual Salary	Annual Salary
1 _____ 9/10	5 _____ 9/10	9 _____ 9/10	13 _____ 9/10
2 _____ 9/10	6 _____ 9/10	10 _____ 9/10	14 _____ 9/10
3 _____ 9/10	7 _____ 9/10	11 _____ 9/10	15 _____ 9/10
4 _____ 9/10	8 _____ 9/10	12 _____ 9/10	16 _____ 9/10

* Report only full-time staff *with master's degrees from graduate library education programs accredited by ALA.*
Do not repeat salaries reported in Part I.

POSITION TITLE: *Reference/Information Librarian* *

POSITION DESCRIPTION: Locates information for library users or helps users find it in print materials, automated databases, or other sources. Answers questions and gives instruction about the use of the library. Selects materials for the reference collection and general collections.

POSITION TITLE: *(if different from above)* _____

Annual Salary	Annual Salary	Annual Salary	Annual Salary
1 _____ 9/10	4 _____ 9/10	7 _____ 9/10	10 _____ 9/10
2 _____ 9/10	5 _____ 9/10	8 _____ 9/10	11 _____ 9/10
3 _____ 9/10	6 _____ 9/10	9 _____ 9/10	12 _____ 9/10

POSITION TITLE: *Cataloger and/or Classifier* *

POSITION DESCRIPTION: Organizes all types of material purchased by the library. Describes each item in standard format and assigns access points. Assigns subject headings and classification numbers. May use automated systems. May be involved with only descriptive cataloging or only subject cataloging/classification.

POSITION TITLE: *(if different from above)* _____

Annual Salary	Annual Salary	Annual Salary	Annual Salary
1 _____ 9/10	3 _____ 9/10	5 _____ 9/10	7 _____ 9/10
2 _____ 9/10	4 _____ 9/10	6 _____ 9/10	8 _____ 9/10

POSITION TITLE: *Children's and/or Young Adult Services Librarian* *

POSITION DESCRIPTION: Plans and conducts library services for children and/or young adults. Advises on reading materials. Selects materials for the collection. May plan and conduct special programs and outreach services.

POSITION TITLE: *(if different from above)* _____

Annual Salary	Annual Salary	Annual Salary	Annual Salary
1 _____ 9/10	3 _____ 9/10	5 _____ 9/10	7 _____ 9/10
2 _____ 9/10	4 _____ 9/10	6 _____ 9/10	8 _____ 9/10

---

* Report only full-time staff *with master's degrees from graduate library education programs accredited by ALA.* Do not repeat salaries reported in Part I.

Part III. SUPPLEMENTARY QUESTIONS

1. Is there a single position on your staff with primary responsibility for many or all of the following duties related to library technology?
    - Recommend policies for automation
    - Plan for the installation of a system
    - Evaluate/select system hardware/software
    - Work with agencies outside the library
    - Test the installed systems
    - Plan site preparation (space, electric, A/C, etc.)
    - Evaluate systems/applications software
    - Trouble shoot system malfunctions
    - Install/configure hardware/software
    - Document system implementation, changes, etc.
    - Oversee the daily operation of the system
    - Participate in the preparation of an RFP
    - Analyze system/user interaction
    - Authorize expenditures for hardware/software
    _____ Yes (please continue)
    _____ No (please skip to A below)

2. What is the title of this position? _____

3. Is the position one of the following:
    _____ Deputy/Associate/Assistant Director
    _____ Department Head
    _____ none of the above

4. Does the current incumbent have a master's degree from a program accredited by ALA? ___Yes ___No

5. What annual salary is paid to the current incumbent? $_____ per year

---

A. Name and title of respondent **: _____

B. Telephone number: (   ) _____

** Neither libraries nor individuals will be identified in the report of this survey. The name of your library is given here so that we can avoid sending reminders to libraries who respond. The name and phone number of the person responding are requested because we may need to contact him or her if we have questions about this return.

THANK YOU VERY MUCH! Please return by **April 18, 1994** in the enclosed postage paid envelope to:

American Library Association
Office for Research and Statistics
50 E. Huron Street
Chicago, Illinois 60611

PLACE LABEL HERE

Appendix G

Salaries Paid for Less Than a Twelve Month Year in Academic Libraries

Instructions on the questionnaire told the respondent: If the incumbent works **less** than a 12-month year (including vacation), please report the salary and circle the appropriate number of months (9 or 10) for which the salary is paid.

A program was written to prorate these salaries to their twelve month equivalents for the purpose of reporting results of this survey. Table G was created to show how often this process was necessary. The first column shows the total number of incumbents for which salaries are reported in each of the three types of academic institutions on the position tables in this report. The second column shows how many were reported as being for nine months and the third column shows the percentage of incumbents in the category (position/type of library) which that number represents. The following columns repeat that pattern for positions reported as being for ten months and then for a combination of nine and ten month salaries.

Table G.

	Salaries Paid for Less Than a 12-month Year in Academic Libraries by Position and Type						
	ALL INCUMBENTS	9-MONTH		10-MONTH		9 AND 10 MONTH	
POSITION AND TYPE OF LIBRARY	#	#	%	#	%	#	%
Director							
Two-year college	130	8	6	11	8	19	15
Four-year college	120	5	4	4	3	9	8
University	240			6	3	6	3
Deputy/Associate/Assistant Director							
Two-year college	35	2	6	2	6	4	11
Four-year college	43	3	7	1	2	4	9
University	334	1		3	1	4	1
Department Head/Branch Head							
Two-year college	67	10	15	1	1	11	16
Four-year college	95	1	1	12	13	13	14
University	1183	14	1	10	1	24	2
Reference/Information Librarian							
Two-year college	156	21	13	43	28	64	41
Four-year college	129	13	10	9	7	22	17
University	1062	23	2	40	4	63	6
Cataloger and/or Classifier							
Two-year college	62	12	19	7	11	19	31
Four-year college	69	6	9	4	6	10	14
University	498	8	2	14	3	22	4